Key Performance Indicators

Steven M. Bragg

AccountingTools®

ISBN 978-1-64221-300-3

For more information about AccountingTools® products, visit our Web site at www.accountingtools.com.

Table of Contents

About the Author

Steven Bragg, CPA, has been the chief financial officer or controller of four companies, as well as a consulting manager at Ernst & Young. He received a master's degree in finance from Bentley College, an MBA from Babson College, and a Bachelor's degree in Economics from the University of Maine. He has been a two-time president of the Colorado Mountain Club, and is an avid alpine skier, mountain biker, and certified master diver. Mr. Bragg resides in Centennial, Colorado. He has written more than 300 books and courses, including *New Controller Guidebook*, *GAAP Guidebook*, and *Payroll Management*.

Steven maintains the accountingtools.com web site, which contains continuing professional education courses, the Accounting Best Practices podcast, and thousands of articles on accounting subjects.

Key Performance Indicators

Introduction

Many businesses fail because management is not clear about where it should focus its attention. This happens because they are buried under an avalanche of to-do items and therefore focus on whatever is directly in front of them, rather than concentrating on those few items that really matter to the business.

An organization should have a measurement system that is closely tied to its critical success factors and strategy, on the theory that only what is measured will be improved by the organization. In this manual, we describe key performance indicators, how they should be developed and integrated into a business, and many related issues.

The Key Performance Indicator

A key performance indicator (KPI) is a core metric used by a business to monitor its progress toward achieving key goals and financial outcomes. It can be useful to break down this concept by each element of its name, as follows:

- *Key.* It is a major contributor to the success or failure of the business.
- *Performance.* It is a metric that can be measured and controlled, so it can be improved over time.
- *Indicator.* It is a reasonable representation of present and future company performance.

In brief, a KPI can be used to drastically increase performance, or lead to the accomplishment of stated objectives. It likely has the following characteristics:

- *Actionable.* The organization clearly understands the corrective actions associated with it in order to improve performance.
- *Clear responsibility.* Someone within the organization is responsible for it. Ideally, it should be tied to the activities of a specific group within the organization.
- *Frequent measurements.* It is measured on a frequent basis, such as hourly, daily, or weekly. If the measurement period is longer than that, it is too late for anyone to take any meaningful corrective action.
- *Major impact.* It is a leading indicator of performance that improves the value of the business. Thus, any steps taken to improve the KPI will also enhance the results of the business.
- *Measurable.* The KPI is based on a standard set of definitions, rules, and calculations, so that it can be consistently measured over time.
- *Minimal negative effects.* Any negative behavioral impacts of the KPI on employees and business partners is minimal.

- *Non-financial.* It is not financial in nature, since financial reporting is focused more on past results than future performance.
- *Simplicity.* It is simple enough to be understood by everyone associated with it. Any degree of complexity muddies the nature of the measurement.

Tip: Pay particular attention to whether a proposed KPI is financial in nature. If so, the person advocating for its usage has probably not drilled down into the situation deeply enough to understand that there are operational activities underlying the proposed KPI that are actually more important to the business.

Tip: A good KPI focuses on exceptions, so that the organization is immediately notified of problems and then acts to correct them. Thus, a KPI that targets customer service calls dropped today is much better than one that measures the proportion of customer service calls that were answered.

EXAMPLE

Suture Corporation engages in the electronic remediation of cancer. Its president recently suggested to a consultant that it designate revenue as a KPI. The consultant points out that revenue is only the outcome of a number of actions, such as sales calls to existing hospital clients and new ones, as well as targeted advertising and the use of existing customers as referral clients – all of which would be better targets as KPIs.

Here are several metrics that would qualify as KPIs, based on the preceding list of characteristics:

- *Airline* – The number of plane arrivals today that are more than 15 minutes late.
- *Consulting* – The number of job offers outstanding today that have been open at least a week.
- *Distributor* – The number of remaining obsolete inventory items today that have not yet been dispositioned.
- *Hospital* – The number of initiatives completed today in response to a customer satisfaction survey.
- *Restaurant* – The number of chefs who have resigned in the past day.
- *Retail store* – The number of customer complaints not resolved today.
- *Software developer* – The number of projects today with slipped completion dates.
- *Supplier* – the number of late deliveries today to key customers.

Note: A common element in the preceding example KPIs is that they are measured daily. If a measurement is not compiled at that level of frequency, then it is probably not sufficiently important to the organization to be a KPI.

As indicated within the preceding list of sample KPIs, most KPIs are derived from current events – that is, they *just* happened. In addition, a business may need to keep track of future KPIs – generally involving the schedule of events that will impact the company in the near future, such as:

- The dates of scheduled visits to *key* customers
- The dates when *key* new products are scheduled for release
- The dates when the new warehouse management system is expected to go live, which will increase the on-time delivery rate to *key* customers

KPIs will vary by industry, due to differences in their operational and financial structures. For example, a warehouse could measure fulfillment days, while a retail store could measure customer returns, a website could measure page views, a human resources department could track gender diversity, a call center could measure employee turnover, and a hospital could track emergency room wait times.

Different functions of a business may have different KPIs. For example, the sales manager may be most concerned with lost customer orders, while the production manager focuses on the customer order fulfillment rate, and the customer service manager deals with the number of customer complaints settled on the first contact, as well as the number of customers who hang up while on hold. Further, the marketing manager may monitor the acquisition cost of each incremental customer gained.

KPIs are closely monitored by management, which should take action if a KPI is not in line with expectations. Over time, the goals of a business may change, so that management decides to replace its KPIs with new ones. If so, the performance monitoring systems of the business should be adjusted to refocus employee attention on the new KPIs.

The Key Results Indicator

When devising KPIs, a company might mistakenly choose to instead use a key results indicator (KRI). A KRI provides information about how an entire organization is performing, based on the activities of a combination of many teams, functions, and/or departments. A KRI is always backward-looking, noting the results generated by the business over the past few weeks or months – usually on a trend line. Since these measures are reported relatively infrequently, they are not useful for making alterations to the business. An organization should keep the number of KRIs it tracks down to 10 or less; many organizations track far more, which can overwhelm the firm with too much information. Examples of KRIs are:

- Membership totals for a professional organization
- Net profit
- Return on investment
- Sales

Financial performance measures should nearly always be classified as results indicators, since they are the end result of underlying operational and financial activities.

KRIs are useful for monitoring past performance, but are not to be confused with KPIs, which are used to drive a business forward.

> **Tip:** When the only person responsible for a metric is the company president, it is probably a KRI.

Critical Success Factors

Critical success factors (CSFs) are activities that need to be done well in order for a business to achieve its mission. These are typically operational issues that employees are handling every day, and are the most important items that absolutely, positively must be done correctly. Therefore, CSFs are prioritized above everything else in the business. For example, FedEx exists to deliver parcels to customers on time, so on-time delivery is clearly a CSF for it. Similarly, a guiding principal of any airline is to arrive on time, so that can be considered a CSF. Or, the CSF of a website services company is to maintain up-time for its client's websites of as close to 100% as possible. When companies clearly recognize their CSFs, they focus the bulk of company resources on those CSFs. Examples of other CSFs are:

- Always maintain proper refrigeration temperature in trailers [for a seafood distributor to restaurants]
- Ensure that all players are properly warmed up before game time [for any team sport]
- Expand the sales force with experienced personnel who are profitable within six months [for any company selling direct to customers through a sales force]
- Verify the proper formulation mix prior to production [for a concrete production facility]

There is a strong linkage between CSFs and KPIs. A KPI is nearly always derived from a CSF, since a CSF is so important to the survival of a business. Thus, FedEx could measure the number of instances in which packages were late today as a KPI, while a website services company could measure the amount of website downtime today as a KPI.

The trouble is that many organizations are not clear about what their CSFs are. In these cases, management merely prioritizes the resources of the organization around what they think is important, rather than what really *is* important. When this is the case, it can be quite difficult to decide upon the nature of the corporate KPIs. The best way to do so is to first go through an exercise of identifying CSFs, from which KPIs can then be derived.

> **Tip:** A useful side-effect of identifying CSFs is that you can eliminate any extraneous metrics scattered around the organization that are not related to those CSFs. By definition, if a metric is not associated with a CSF, then it is not very important, and so may be eliminated or at least designated as viable only over the short-term.

KPI Derivation Problems

There are several issues within an organization that can make it more difficult to derive proper KPIs. Here are the concerns to be aware of:

- *No CSF linkage.* A KPI may not be linked to a critical success factor, so using it does not propel the company in the right direction. This may happen when a manager has a favorite KPI and so pushes it even when there are no CSFs to support it.
- *Historical linkage.* The KPI has been used in the past, but may no longer be relevant to the current direction of the business. If this KPI continues to be used, it could result in the diversion of valuable resources away from the strategic needs of the business. This happens when some managers are closely tied to the older processes and profit centers of the business, and want to see them continue.
- *Based on industry benchmark.* The KPI might have been selected from a list of KPIs that similar companies use. This KPI might not have a direct bearing on how the company operates or the direction in which it is going. This situation arises when consultants have taken over the KPI development process.
- *Vague statement.* A KPI may be worded as a vague statement, rather than something that can be measured. For example, "Maintain current levels of operational effectiveness." This sometimes happens when managers do not want to be held to account, and so suggest KPIs that are impossible to measure.

The Difference Between Metrics and KPIs

A common problem is differentiating between metrics and KPIs. Here are several ways to look at the differences:

- *Focus.* Metrics track the status of a business process, while KPIs provide more accurate information about what could happen in the future if present trends continue. KPIs must be relevant to the achievement of specific business targets, which is not necessarily the case with metrics.
- *Frequency.* KPIs tend to be reviewed more frequently than metrics, possibly as frequently as on a daily or hourly basis. Conversely, the tracking of metrics can usually be conducted on a more infrequent basis.
- *Support level.* Metrics support KPIs, while KPIs support the critical success factors and strategy of the business.
- *Volume.* There tend to be far fewer KPIs than metrics. A business might have only a handful of KPIs, but could monitor over a hundred metrics.

For example, a business routinely tracks its inventory turnover percentage and the time required to complete the physical inventory count. Both are metrics, but they are not KPIs, because they only report on processes. Conversely, the daily review of foodstuffs in inventory that are about to spoil can be considered a KPI for a restaurant, since this specific issue can cause the business to lose a massive amount of money if not closely monitored.

Key KPI Considerations

When selecting KPIs, there are a number of issues to consider that have a bearing on the outcome. For example:

- *Accountability*. Who should be responsible for each KPI? Ideally, a KPI should be traceable back to a specific team, which is responsible for it. Conversely, a KPI is not effective when multiple groups are responsible for it, since it is much more difficult to tie the KPI to a specific party.
- *Controllable*. Only pick something that can be influenced by the actions of the company; all KPIs must be controllable. There is no point in measuring an activity if the firm cannot change the outcome.
- *Measurement frequency*. What is a reasonable interval at which to measure KPIs? It should usually be measured frequently, since it is associated with the day-to-day success of the business.
- *Number of KPIs*. What is a reasonable number of KPIs? Too many can lead to a burdensome amount of measurement and reporting activities, while too few represents a lack of critical information. A common result is for a business to have too many KPIs. Generally, six to 10 KPIs can be considered reasonable.
- *Publicity*. To what extent should the organization publicize its KPIs? It could post them for employees to see, such as in public areas and the company newsletter. However, a possible motivational concern is that an adverse KPI outcome can have a negative impact on morale.
- *Replacement*. How frequently should a KPI be replaced? They will lose their impact over time, so they should be periodically reviewed, and replaced as necessary.

KPI Examples

We have listed under the following headings a number of measurements that may be treated as KPIs.

Sales/Marketing/Customer-Related KPIs

- Cancellation of orders by key customers
- Late deliveries to key customers
- Number of initiatives implemented from the latest customer survey
- Call center abandonments (customer gives up)
- Calls on hold longer than __ seconds (for a customer service call line)
- Complaints not resolved during the first phone call from a customer
- Complaints from key customers not resolved within two hours

- Price quotations to key customers taking longer than one day
- Number of negative customer comments on social media left unanswered

Production-Related KPIs

- Key materials expected to be out of stock before the next scheduled delivery date
- Production schedule delays
- Unscheduled downtime at the bottleneck operation
- Quality defects found in products today
- Defective products returned by customers today
- Near-miss incidents that could have caused pollution events
- Amount of emissions from production

Human Resources-Related KPIs

- Number of job offers not accepted that are more than three days old
- Unresolved employee complaints
- Accidents or safety breaches reported today
- Employees who have handed in their notice to leave the company's employment today
- Vehicle fleet traffic accidents reported today

IT-Related KPIs

- Instances of unauthorized access to computer systems
- Key system downtime

Regulatory-Related KPIs

- Warnings received from regulatory agencies

Project-Related KPIs

- Number of assigned resources versus planned resources
- Number of cost revisions
- Number of schedule revisions
- Percent of actual versus planned best practices used
- Percent of work packages adhering to the schedule

The examples noted here should not imply that a simple, aggregate total for each KPI is forwarded to management. Instead, there should be an underlying report associated with each of these KPIs that provides sufficient information for recipients to take action. For example, the KPI for the number of offers not accepted by recruits should have an accompanying report that states the names of these recruits, the time lag since the offer was made, who is responsible for that recruit, and the contact information for the responsible party. With this information in hand, a manager can call up the person in charge and make pointed inquiries about what the person plans to do to correct the situation. As another example, the KPI for employees handing in their notice should have an accompanying report that states the name of this person, his or her job title, length of service with the company, and contact information.

KPI Ranking

Management may come up with a number of KPIs that it wants to track. If so, this can dilute management attention among too many measurements, resulting in few improvements to the business. To prevent this from happening, management needs to prioritize KPIs, so that the most important items are clearly highlighted at the top of the list. This forced ranking shows everyone in the business where to focus the bulk of their time and other resources. This process is not as simple as it may initially appear. Here are several examples of the complexities involved:

- Should the business focus on customer lifetime value, or simply net profits for product lines that are expected to be cancelled within the next few years?
- Should the business focus more on customer satisfaction in those product lines where repeat business is more common, and more on profitability in product lines where there is usually just a single sale per customer?
- How should revenue enhancement be balanced against net promoter scores and general customer satisfaction levels?
- How should the company's pricing policies be balanced against the risk of triggering a regulatory review?
- Over what time horizon should we optimize the value of the business? Is this quite a short-range decision, or are we focusing multiple decades into the future?

A simple optimization of each KPI on a list based on their priority ignores their inherent interdependence. Instead, management needs to balance individual KPIs to optimize the overall strategy of the business. For example, just emphasizing enhanced cash flow does not help a business if its second-priority KPI is to increase the capacity of the bottleneck operation, when doing so requires a large cash investment. In this case, management needs to decide how much cash flow is enough, and then shift the remaining cash above this threshold level to the bottleneck-related KPI. There is no perfect answer – management has to weigh the alternatives and come up with a mix of targeted outcomes.

Misleading KPIs

Management could unintentionally select KPIs that are misleading. For example, many businesses rely on subscribers as the basis for their revenue growth. When this is the case, management might be misled into just tracking the grand total number of subscribers. However, this could mask a great deal of churn among subscribers. A better approach is to track a combination of new subscriber additions within the last few months and the number of subscriber cancellations over the same period. When tracked on a trend line, these two figures can give management a clear idea of how subscriber numbers are actually trending. For example, a declining trend of new subscriber additions and increasing subscriber cancellations is a clear leading indicator for management that corrective action is needed.

Management can also be tripped up by how it defines the information that goes into a KPI. For example, a business might elect to use the book-to-bill ratio as a KPI, which compares the total sales backlog to the revenue recognized within the most recent period; this can be an important leading indicator when tracked on a trend line, since a declining book-to-bill ratio indicates that a business is running out of backlog, which will eventually be reflected in declining sales. However, this ratio could be misleading if cancelable orders are included in the backlog portion of the calculation, or orders in which the purchase quantity is not defined, or where sales contracts allow customers to extend the mandated delivery dates. In these cases, the backlog figure could suddenly collapse as questionable backlog items are subsequently revised. This is a good example of how the numbers going into a KPI need to be carefully evaluated and then strictly locked down, to keep the KPI from providing misleading information to management.

KPI Negative Effects

The use of KPIs will not necessarily improve the results of a business. In many cases, they have unintended negative effects that result in counterproductive behavior by employees, as described in the following examples.

EXAMPLE

A mining operation installs a KPI mandating that the mine elevator deliver 500 miners into the mine at the beginning and end of each shift. However, the elevator is running at reduced speed due to ongoing maintenance issues, so the elevator operator simply runs the miners down to the first level of the mine, because it is the closest level to the surface, and allows for a faster return trip. Doing so allows the elevator operator to meet his miner delivery KPI, but does little for the mine's productivity, since few of the miners are scheduled to work on the first level.

In this case, the KPI has a strong negative effect of delivering miners where they are not needed. A better KPI would have been to fix all elevator maintenance issues within 24 hours of their being reported.

EXAMPLE

The customer service operation of a major software company sets a target of having customers on hold no longer than five minutes. The current wait time is 28 minutes, and management is not giving the customer service manager additional funding for more staff. Accordingly, he sets the phone system to only accept 20 callers into the phone queue; it hangs up on all other callers. By doing so, he immediately meets management's target, and also angers a large number of callers who cannot get through to the customer service department at all.

Here are several reasons why KPIs can have negative effects:

- Responsibility for a KPI is assigned at too low a level of responsibility within the organization, where there is little power to improve it.
- A KPI is not directly related to the strategy or objectives of the business, so that improving it does not enhance the business. In some cases, it may even contravene the strategy of the business.
- The rate at which the KPI can be changed is too slow, so that even extensive efforts will only improve it over a relatively long period of time.
- There are so many KPIs being measured that employees are confused about where to direct their attention.
- Certain managers are directing that certain easily achievable metrics be designated as KPIs, so that they can more easily earn performance-based bonuses.

EXAMPLE

The board of directors of Pianoforte International, maker of concert-grade pianos, wants to take the company in a new direction, focusing on self-playing upright pianos that can be tucked away discretely in a larger home. Accordingly, it sets a KPI of focusing on unit sales of these new machines, to be reported to the company president every day.

However, management wants the R&D group to complete work on the company's latest concert grand piano before completing the development of the new self-playing units. This project was the focus of a KPI in the prior year. As a result of management's actions, the new KPI shows zero activity for the first half-year, as resources continue to be directed toward the old, defunct KPI relating to the concert grand piano project.

A further negative effect can arise when the cost of data collection to calculate a KPI is too high, either in terms of actual monetary cost or employee time. In either case, employees may try to find shortcuts to collect the necessary data or do so less frequently; either situation damages the reliability of the resulting KPI. The best way to deal with this situation is to review in advance the difficulty of creating and updating each KPI; an unusually poor cost/benefit ratio may lead management to search for an alternative KPI. Examples of measurements that typically have a poor cost/benefit ratio are:

- Number of business opportunities added/lost today
- Time required to complete a key process
- Time spent on personal development activities

The preceding examples all require ongoing tracking by employees, which they find annoying, and will try to evade whenever possible.

KPI Software

During the first few months of a KPI installation, the use of electronic spreadsheets to formulate KPI results is sufficient, since the KPIs are still being evaluated to see if they will work for the company, and the underlying calculations may require tweaking. Also, using spreadsheets early on eliminates any delays associated with having to evaluate and select more specialized software. At this stage, the main point is simply to get the system running.

Once the KPIs to be used have been firmly decided upon (probably after a number of months have passed), management can then initiate an evaluation process to obtain a business analytics software package. This package is used to collect the information needed to calculate its KPIs, and presents up-to-date results to management through a dashboard that is available on their computers. The system should ideally be able to report KPI updates at least on a fixed schedule, such as the start of work each morning, if not in real time for specific incidents. The latest versions of these packages should be able to push KPI results out to the smart phones of users, in a coherent graphical display format.

> **Note:** Electronic spreadsheets should not be considered a long-term reporting tool for KPIs, since they are subject to incorrect formulas, broken links, incorrect or missing data items, and a general lack of control.

The business analytics software can also be used to compile key results indicators, usually at longer intervals than for KPIs. These KRI reports can then be distributed as necessary, such as to management, the board of directors, and external stakeholders. The board does not need to see KPI results, since their role is governance, not management.

> **Tip:** The display of KPI information should be structured to exclude excessive clutter, with KPIs clustered by common topic, and red coloration being used to highlight areas of concern. Pie charts and 3-D charts are more difficult to read, and so should be banned from the presentation.

KPIs Relating to Artificial Intelligence

It is possible that artificial intelligence (AI) may be of considerable use to many organizations in improving their competitive edge. When this is the case, management needs to evaluate how AI will play a role in determining which KPIs are measured. AI can then be specifically targeted at optimizing the chosen KPIs. For example, Uber and Lyft use AI to optimize their ride-sharing platforms, so that they can more accurately estimate arrival times for their passengers – which is one of their KPIs. Customers need to have an accurate estimated time of arrival for their drivers, so that they can more accurately schedule their journeys inside an Uber or Lyft vehicle.

AI can be used to sort through massive amounts of social media data to search for comments about a business, which can be used to develop a KPI regarding customer satisfaction with the business. At a more advanced level, AI can learn to identify emergent KPIs that are not yet obvious to management. In this latter case, the AI is essentially distilling the data to learn what the KPIs should be. It is entirely possible that these AI-derived KPIs are ones that a company might never have spotted on its own.

In order to use AI most effectively, a business needs access to significant quantities of high-volume data through which the AI can churn. To obtain it, a business needs to recognize which types of data will be most useful for the identification and ongoing analysis of KPIs. This calls for a staff of data scientists who can collect and clean data, as well as analyze the results returned by the corporate AI.

KPI Implementation Activities

Given the negative issues noted in the earlier sections of this manual, it makes sense to work through a standard implementation drill to ensure that the negative effects associated with a KPI are minimized. The implementation can be encapsulated into a four-step process, which is as follows:

1. Obtain commitment from the company to install KPIs. This involves selling the KPI project to senior management, obtaining funding, and then assembling a team that will run the KPI project.
2. Determine the critical success factors of the business. Run a workshop with key employees to decide what critical success factors the company has.
3. Identify KPIs. Initially identify a range of possible KPIs and then narrow down the field to arrive at a small number of final KPIs.
4. Implement the KPIs. Design a system for collecting information about the KPIs and reporting them to management. Follow up on this system as appropriate to make adjustments to it.

Even when this process is followed exactly as indicated, it is quite possible that the KPI project will still fail, because management did not address several underlying issues, which are:

- *Internal and external support.* All parts of the business need to be behind the KPI effort, which means management, employees, customers, and suppliers. This is easiest when everyone involved sees a need for change; usually because the business is currently experiencing some problems.
- *Front line empowerment.* KPIs can be improved most effectively when people low in the corporate hierarchy are empowered to take action. This results in actions being taken much more quickly than if all decisions are routed up to the management committee, which can take days or weeks for a response.
- *Minimized reporting.* The business should only assemble data into reports and issue them when doing so is essential to the organization. Otherwise, adding new KPIs to the mix will ensure that they are lost in the sea of other metrics already being spread around through the organization. A side effect is that the business should routinely eliminate metrics that are not helping it, or which result in dysfunctional performance.

- *Derived from CSFs.* All KPIs should be derived from the critical success factors of the business, since those CSFs keep the organization in business. Conversely, any metric *not* linked to a CSF probably does not qualify as a KPI.
- *Operated internally.* The process of devising KPIs and implementing them should be managed by someone in-house on a full-time basis, as opposed to a consultant. This person has the best knowledge of how the organization works, its critical success factors, and how to ensure that new KPIs will be accepted.

EXAMPLE

Cajun Delights Restaurant is adopting a KPI of ensuring rapid table turnover at all of its locations. It soon realizes that this KPI will not improve unless it gains the agreement of its food supplier, since that supplier must increase the number of food deliveries in order to ensure that the kitchens never run short of food.

EXAMPLE

The Roll Tide retail store chain, purveyor of all things involving the University of Alabama, decides to implement a KPI for unresolved customer complaints. Senior management soon finds that the only way to improve this KPI is to empower the individual store clerks to settle all issues on the spot, such as offering discounts for damaged merchandise and allowing product returns even for items where the customer has no receipt.

EXAMPLE

Rubens Trailers manufactures double wide trailers for the rotund. The company controller insists on producing a vast array of reports on every variance from the company's highly detailed annual budget, along with itemizations of the underlying causes. The recipients spend hours investigating these variances and then reporting their action plans back to the executive committee. Given that this system leaves no time to deal with a new set of KPIs, the president tells the controller to limit his reporting to only the largest variances, which eliminates 95% of the reporting.

EXAMPLE

A critical success factor of the Lethal Sushi restaurant chain is ensuring that its chefs are properly trained, since an improperly prepared blowfish can kill a customer. Consequently, it adopts the associated KPI of how long it has been since a trained chef quit the kitchen, so that management can immediately initiate a search for a qualified replacement.

EXAMPLE

Eldritch Jones, the controller of Rio Shipping, is tasked with developing and implementing a set of KPIs for this international freight shipping company. However, he is also deeply involved in installing new accounting software and the process of taking the company public, and so makes no progress on the task for three months. He finally shifts the task over to a long-time assistant controller who has deep knowledge of how the company operates; she is assigned to this task exclusively, and so is able to complete the work in a few months.

Several additional points pertaining to the implementation process are as follows:

- *Initial support*. The initial support for a KPI project can be surprisingly difficult to obtain, because the company will see this initiative as simply the need to come up with yet more metrics upon which they will be judged. A better environment in which to expect support is when the company is going through a troubled period, and recognizes that *something* needs to change – thereby providing some initial support for the KPI concept.
- *CEO support*. The chief executive officer of the company should be driving the KPI initiative. This means that the KPI team should be reporting directly to the CEO. When this is not the case, it is a warning flag that the CEO does not fully support the project.
- *Coalition building*. KPIs are especially difficult to implement, because they impact the entire organization, and so require broad-based support. To achieve this, spend a significant amount of time up-front, selling the concept to a coalition of key influencers within the organization. These people are in a position to influence others, and so are essential drivers of the implementation process.
- *Team composition*. The KPI team should be comprised of experienced staff who fully understand the critical success factors of the business, and who have the right mix of experience, knowledge, and credibility within the organization to enhance the success of the project.
- *Consulting support*. The KPI team should be supported by a KPI consultant who understands how the process should flow and where the pitfalls lie. Ideally, this person should have already worked on a number of KPI engagements.
- *Facilitation support*. Hire a facilitator who is experienced in assisting businesses in developing KPIs. This person should facilitate a series of meetings in which possible KPIs are explored, after which the final KPIs are selected.
- *Staff support*. Employees will be more likely to support the project if you emphasize that focusing on the right metrics will make their work more effective, since it is more closely linked to the corporate strategy. In addition, the KPIs may enhance the profitability of the business, which should improve their job security.
- *Pilot project*. Consider initially rolling out a KPI as a pilot project, to see how employees react to it. In a larger business, rolling out a KPI within just one

subsidiary can be considered a pilot project. If employee behavior is negatively impacted, then adjust the KPI and try again, or shut it down entirely and try a different KPI. When this happens, be sure to document the outcome, so that management can incorporate this experience into the development of other KPIs.

- *Quick wins.* Whenever possible, try to implement some portion of the project quickly, so that the organization sees the KPIs project as succeeding. This builds support, especially if a series of these quick wins can be scheduled over the course of the project.
- *Communications.* Since a KPI project impacts the entire organization, it is essential to continually communicate project progress to everyone, many times over, through as many different media as possible. This could include presentations, emails, newsletters, and even impromptu updates during meetings intended for other purposes.
- *Compensation linkage.* Should KPIs should be linked to employee compensation? This is generally not a good idea, since it incentivizes employees to do whatever it takes, including incorrect calculation of the KPIs, to achieve favorable outcomes. A better approach is to recognize employees in non-monetary ways for their work in improving KPIs.
- *Weeding out.* If there are detractors who refuse to support the new KPIs, it may be necessary to remove them from any positions in which they can cause the effort to fail.

Subsequent Events

Once a complete set of KPIs has been installed, there are a few additional tasks to be aware of on an ongoing basis. They are:

- *CEO contacts.* The chief executive officer is expected to contact responsible parties on an ongoing basis whenever a KPI indicates a problem. By doing so, the entire organization realizes that this is an important issue for the CEO, which will increase the level of attention it receives.
- *KPI training.* The company should mandate that new employees be required to attend a training class in KPIs, so that they recognize the importance of these measures, how the measures are compiled and calculated, and how they are expected to react to any problems indicated by the KPIs.
- *New metric approvals.* If there are any proposals to add new metrics, they must be approved by the person or team left in charge of the KPI project. Without this approval, it is quite likely that a morass of new metrics will proliferate throughout the organization, diluting the focus on the core set of KPIs.
- *Non-reporting incidents.* Flag any cases in which KPIs are not being properly reported in a timely manner, since this omission can keep the management team from acting promptly on critical success factors.

- *Periodic CSF updates*. Management should periodically review its critical success factors to see if they are still valid. Some are likely to be quite long-term in nature, while others can be periodically swapped out for new ones.
- *Periodic KPI updates*. There should be at least an annual review of the existing KPIs to see if they are still valid, or if some should be swapped out for other KPIs that better reflect the critical success factors of the business. Also, negative effects associated with certain KPIs may come to light, which mandate different reporting options.

Summary

Employees are more likely to perform well in those areas being monitored closely with key performance indicators, which means that KPIs have an outsized impact on the organization. That being the case, management should exercise great care in identifying the best possible KPIs, and then structuring the related reporting system to ensure that KPI issues are brought to the attention of responsible parties as soon as possible. Doing so greatly improves the chances that the organization will continue to be competitive and profitable for a long time to come.

Glossary

C

Critical success factor. An activity that needs to be done well in order for a business to achieve its mission.

K

Key performance indicator. A core metric used by a business to monitor its progress toward achieving key goals and financial outcomes.

Key results indicator. A metric that provides information about how an entire organization is performing, based on the activities of a combination of many teams, functions, and/or departments.

M

Metrics. Measurements of quantitative assessment that are used to track performance.

Index

www.ingramcontent.com/pod-product-compliance
Lightning Source LLC
Chambersburg PA
CBHW051432200326
41520CB00023B/7446